For more information look up the following:

Belle W. Baruch Institute for Marine and Costal Sciences, Georgetown, South Carolina

The Riverbanks Zoo and Botanical Garden, Columbia, South Carolina

Roper Mountain Science Center, Greenville, South Carolina

South Carolina Department of Natural Resources

The Audubon Society

Woodrow Wilson
Wood Stork

Dedicated to Peyton and Nick, my precious grandchildren who make me feel young when we play together in the very creek that Woodrow waded in, searching for food.

Special thanks goes to Greg Cornwell from Roper Mountain Science Center in Greenville, SC. He knew the resources needed to save Woodrow and was able to put them all into action, saving this beautiful bird.

A huge thank you to Valerie Gaumont for editing this book. As an accomplished author it took her skills to make some of my words more interesting than when I first put them on paper. Also, to Roy Sabean who is a true artist and brought Woodrow to life on paper.

The Amazing Travels Of Woodrow Wilson Wood Stork

If Only....

"If I only had today to do over again, I wouldn't be in trouble. Why can't I learn things easier than I do? Is there something wrong with me that every lesson is a hard one? When mom asked me to fly around and bring home something to eat, how was I to know that the pretty colored snake was poisonous? She really didn't have to get so upset yelling at me about the snake. I'm going to fly and fly and stay out all night and make her sorry she yelled at me!" Woodrow Wilson Wood Stork sure had a lot to think about as he flew farther and farther from home.

Hours went by! Days went by! Woodrow didn't know exactly how many, 2, 1, 5, 8, 3, 10. "I guess I still need to work on my numbers," he thought to himself. "Boy, am I hungry! I could eat a whole marsh of minnows," was all he could think of. Missing his mom was replaced by the need for food and rest. He had no idea where he was. "Am I still in Charleston or one of those cities nearby?" he said to himself. What had he learned about the state of South Carolina? He knew that Columbia was the capital but what other places were nearby? He just knew that he wasn't in Charleston anymore because the weather had gotten much cooler and he hadn't seen a palmetto tree in a long time.

"I really need to eat and rest. If I could only
find a cypress tree to land in and rest my wings
for awhile," he thought. Just then he looked
down and saw a small area covered with water
where ducks swam and turtles sun-bathed on a
log. He thought to himself that perhaps a nice
turtle dinner would really hit the spot.
Unfortunately as he landed on the pond, the
turtles dove into the water, much too deep for
him to follow. Unknown to Woodrow was the
fact that if he didn't find some food quickly, he
might not make it one more day.

The Encounter

He started to move toward the shallow water, where the creek flowed into the pond. He had no idea how long he moved his feet along the sandy bottom, trying to stir up something to eat. By the height of the sun, his instincts told him that the time was close to noon. All of a sudden Woodrow found himself in a large shadow. "Must be a cloud or something," he thought to himself. The 'something' turned out to be two human adults and three human children.

"HUMANS, HUMANS," set off an alarm in his head. His little heart thumped so loudly and quickly that he could actually hear the beats. All he could think of was ESCAPE! This plan was quickly put aside as he realized that he was too weak to do anything except let the lady human pick him up out of the water and carry him up the hill to their human nest.

What did she think she was doing carrying a wood stork? After all, he had been told humans believed that wood storks carried baby humans to their new home. All of a sudden, the human lady threw him up in the air. I guess she thought this would get him to fly. NOT!!! "What am I going to do?" He thought. "I need to get away from them because they are the enemy. Haven't they invaded our habitats and destroyed our wetland?"

The Rescue

Before he knew what was happening, Woodrow was placed in some type of cage and the children, Windy, Dwight and Heather, were feeding him minnows, lots and lots of minnows! Woodrow realized that these humans weren't going to hurt him, but that they were actually trying to help him. He knew he had trouble with numbers but it sure seemed like there was one more human adult looking at him. This new human, Greg, told the others that they had a wood stork in their cage and that he was on the endangered species list. "I wonder what this 'endangered' means," thought Woodrow. "Whatever it means, I think I must be pretty important."

Woodrow had just started to relax and feel safe and satisfied from his great meal of minnows when he found himself being put into a box. "Don't these humans know that I'm supposed to be in a cypress tree and not a cardboard box?" What Woodrow didn't understand was that he was going to be placed, box and all, inside a helicopter and flown all the way to the Riverbanks Zoo in Columbia, South Carolina

"Hey, who turned out the lights? It's dark in here," screamed Woodrow. "What's happening to me? Somebody work with me here! I've got a beak and I'm not afraid to use it," he yelled in stork talk. Like it or not, Woodrow was continuing on his great adventure, but all he really wanted was to be protected by his mom and dad in the family nest. What else could possibly happen to him?

The box, with Woodrow inside, was placed in a truck and driven away, but to where? Woodrow kept wondering just where he was headed. He used his beak to peck out a hole in the box. When the truck stopped, he looked out his little hole and saw a sign but didn't understand what it meant – South Carolina Department of Natural Resources. Not far from where the truck had stopped was a loud, funny looking bird. This bird was huge! It had no feathers! It was shiny and its wings were in all the wrong places! The humans picked up Woodrow's box and placed it inside the monster bird.

Before he could say "There's no place like home!" Woodrow was airborne. Now Woodrow was used to flying but under his own power, not in a make believe, loud, featherless bird with wings in all the wrong places. He hadn't been flying for too long when the strange bird landed and Woodrow was placed in another truck. In no time at all he was also put into another cage. Everything was scary and strange. Woodrow just couldn't understand that all that was being done to him was being done to help him. The humans were trying to save him, not hurt him.

The Rehabilitation

Woodrow spent the next few weeks at the Riverbanks Zoo being looked after and most importantly, fed. He gained the necessary weight and was looked after by animal doctors called veterinarians. One day he recognized the human that had placed him into the box a few weeks ago. How could Woodrow know that this man, Greg, was part of a group called The Audubon Society and that he was trying to do anything that could be done to save Woodrow. Woodrow came to realize that when this man was around he was going places! Sure enough, he was on the move again! What Woodrow didn't know was that this would be the last time a human would ever move him around.

The Farewell

The humans went with him on this, the last part of his journey. When Woodrow was taken out of the box, he could not believe his eyes. He was at a place called the Bell W. Baruch Institute for Marine and Coastal Sciences. He saw a lot of wood storks wading in the water. Their eyes were all focused on him. He was a bit nervous as he waded closer and closer to the others like him. He would have to start right away trying to make new friends. Woodrow could not find his father, mother, sisters or brothers. This wasn't the home he once knew; but when Woodrow looked around and saw turtles and minnows in the marshy waters, he had a feeling it would be a comfortable place to live. He didn't know if he would see his family again; but he had grown up a lot in the last few months. He knew that there were humans interested in helping endangered birds like him, so that there would always be wood storks gracing their skies. He felt grateful to the humans who helped to save him and hoped more people would protect wetlands for them to live in and raise their families.

He had been so absorbed in his thoughts that he didn't realize the humans had all moved away from him, giving Woodrow the chance to move on. He turned around and gave these special people a farewell look and wondered if they could understand his gratitude. Turning back toward the other wood storks, he moved forward with his feet as well as his life!

Questions for "If Only...."

1. What is Woodrow's problem?

2. Why did his mom get so upset?

3. How do you think he is feeling?

Questions for "The Encounter"

1. Why did Woodrow land where he did?

2. Why was he so scared?

3. What do you think the humans had done to become the enemy?

Questions for "The Rescue"

1. Did the humans help Woodrow?

2. How did they help?

3. Why did Woodrow have to be put into the box?

Questions for "The Rehabilitation"

1. Would you be scared to ride in a helicopter?

2. Was Woodrow starting to trust the humans?

3. Why would a flying bird be afraid to fly?

Questions for "The Farewell"

1. What type of place do you think they took Woodrow to?

2. Do you think Woodrow will daydream again and get lost?

3. Have you ever thought about how you might help an animal? Always check with your parents first.

www.ingramcontent.com/pod-product-compliance
Lightning Source LLC
Chambersburg PA
CBHW070457290526
45791CB00005B/2149